KAREN LATCHANA KENNEY

THE SCIENCE OF COLOR

INVESTIGATING LIGHT

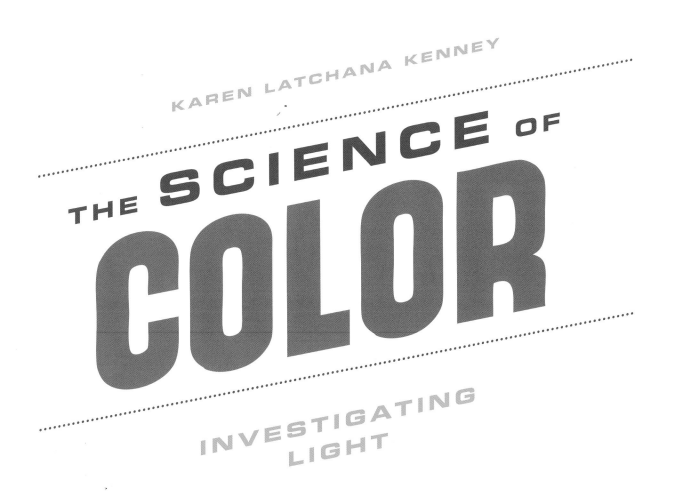

Checkerboard Library

An Imprint of Abdo Publishing
abdopublishing.com

abdopublishing.com

Published by Abdo Publishing, a division of ABDO, PO Box 398166, Minneapolis, Minnesota 55439. Copyright © 2016 by Abdo Consulting Group, Inc. International copyrights reserved in all countries. No part of this book may be reproduced in any form without written permission from the publisher. Checkerboard Library™ is a trademark and logo of Abdo Publishing.

Printed in the United States of America, North Mankato, Minnesota

102015
012016

THIS BOOK CONTAINS
RECYCLED MATERIALS

Design: Christa Schneider
Production: Mighty Media, Inc.
Editor: Rebecca Felix

Cover Photos: Shutterstock, front cover, back cover
Interior Photos: Mighty Media, Inc., pp. 4-5, 7, 11, 17, 21; NIST, p. 25; Shutterstock, pp. 6, 8, 9, 13, 14, 15, 16, 17, 19, 20, 22, 23, 24, 26, 27, 28–29

Library of Congress Cataloging-in-Publication Data

Kenney, Karen Latchana, author.
  The science of color : investigating light / by Karen Latchana Kenney.
    pages cm. -- (Science in action)
  Includes index.
  ISBN 978-1-62403-960-7
1. Color--Juvenile literature. 2. Light--Wave-length--Juvenile literature. 3. Optics--Juvenile literature. I. Title.
  QC495.5.K456 2016
  535.6--dc23
                    2015026276

CONTENTS

SUDDENLY...
A RAINBOW!

Heavy rain drips slowly to a stop. The storm is over and the air is heavy with water. Behind you, dark clouds part to reveal gleaming beams of sunlight. Suddenly, a stack of red, orange, yellow, green, blue, indigo, and violet arches across the sky.

The rainbow seems to appear out of nowhere. But its colors are split from the sun's white light.

Mixed into the stormy sky are water droplets. Each droplet acts as a tiny **prism**. Sunlight enters a droplet. The light appears white, but it actually contains seven colors combined. Light is always moving, but it slows down in water and bends. It bounces off the other side of the droplet. The light's colors separate as it bends again. A rainbow exits the droplet!

WHAT IS COLOR?

CHAPTER 1

Have you noticed you can't see colors outdoors at night? That's because visible light is the key to color. Visible light is made up of red, orange, yellow, green, blue, indigo, and violet.

The moon does not create visible light.

As light hits an object, some of the light is absorbed. Some of the light is reflected. That reflected light contains a color. We see the object as having this reflected color.

Each color moves in a wave of energy. Some waves have high peaks and low valleys. Others move in lower hills and valleys. From one peak, or high point, to the next high point is the **wavelength**. The different colors in visible light all have different wavelengths.

THE ELECTROMAGNETIC SPECTRUM

SPECTRUM OF VISIBLE LIGHT

ENERGY

WAVELENGTH

Visible light is just one part of the energy the sun **emits**. An entire **spectrum**, or range, of energy comes from the sun. It is called the **electromagnetic** spectrum. At the low end of the spectrum, the energy has long, slow **wavelengths**. At the high end of the spectrum, the energy has very short, fast wavelengths. We cannot see all energies on the spectrum. We can only see visible light.

The energy wavelengths are measured in **nanometers**. Visible light is near the middle of the spectrum. The colors closer to the spectrum's low end, such as red, have slower wavelengths. The colors closer to the spectrum's high end, such as violet, have faster wavelengths.

TRAVELING
LIGHT

Feel the sun's heat warm your face. Watch as its light glitters on a sandy beach. What you feel and see is energy. Its source is the sun, our planet's fiery star, and a giant ball of energy. Nearly everything on Earth needs the sun's energy to live and grow. And all things need the sun's light energy to be visible.

The sun's energy hitting the earth creates many effects. Colors become visible. Water sparkles. Its surface warms too.

The sun's super-hot core can reach a sizzling 27 million degrees Fahrenheit (15 million°C)!

The sun is made up mainly of hydrogen atoms. And it is very hot. Its temperatures are so high they cause **nuclear fusion**. This causes hydrogen atoms to fuse together. The chemical reaction of the atoms fusing releases a huge amount of energy. That energy is released into space in every direction. As it travels, some of the energy lands on Earth in many forms. Light is the visible form of this energy.

RADIATING WAVES

Light has a lot of distance to cover before we see it.
The sun is nearly 93 million miles (150 million km) away
from Earth! But light travels very fast, at 186,000 miles
(299,000 km) per second. That's called the speed of
light. Even moving this fast, light takes 8.33 minutes to
travel from the sun to Earth.

Have you seen sunlight beam toward you at sunrise?
These beams appear to the human eye as straight lines.
But as we have seen, light actually travels in waves.

Light is a type of **electromagnetic radiation**. It is
made of electric and magnetic fields joined together.
Within light are tiny particles called photons that are
electrically charged. This stream of particle energy
moves in waves.

Though these waves move in different directions, the
stream **ultimately** travels forward in straight lines. And
because the human eye cannot see its waves of energy,
we see the sunbeam as a straight line.

Did you also notice the shadow behind you during sunrise? Your body creates a shadow by blocking some sunlight from reaching the ground. Why doesn't the light just travel around you? Because light only bounces and reflects off reflective surfaces. Your body is not reflective. That is why your body can block some light.

AN ELECTROMAGNETIC WAVE

An electric field joins with a magnetic field to make an **electromagnetic** wave. The fields are connected at an angle but move in the same forward direction.

DIRECTION OF STREAM

ELECTRIC FIELD

MAGNETIC FIELD

WHITE LIGHT

The light that reaches the Earth is called white light. But white light is not white. It appears to the human eye to have no color at all. But white light is not colorless either! The full color **spectrum** exists within white light: red, orange, yellow, green, blue, indigo, and violet. Why can't people see these colors directly as light streams from the sun?

Remember, each color in light moves in a different **wavelength**. Have you ever wondered why the colors of a rainbow appear in a certain order? This is because of the length of each color's wavelengths.

Red and violet are the two outer colors. Red is the longest, or slowest wavelength. It measures around 700 nanometers.

The shortest wavelength in the spectrum belongs to the color violet. This wavelength measures around

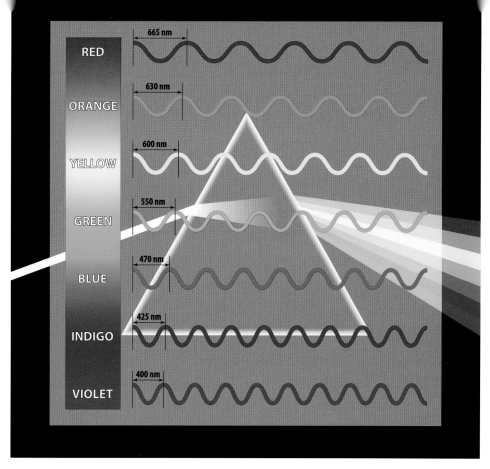

When the combination of each color's wavelengths hits the human eye at once, we see the color white.

400 nanometers. The colors in between go in order by length of wavelength.

When light comes directly from the sun, all colors' **wavelengths** are mixed together. The colors blend and we cannot pick out one color within the light. To see the different colors, the wavelengths need to be separated.

SEPARATING COLORS

Water drops are one way light's colors can be separated. The drops act as a **prism**. Other items can act as prisms too. Have you ever hung a crystal **suncatcher** in a sunny window? Did you see tiny rainbows scatter around the room? The crystal suncatcher is made to be a prism. It separates **wavelengths** of the colors mixed within sunlight.

There are different types of prisms. A simple prism has three sides and three angles. It is made of a **transparent** material, such as glass.

When sunlight enters the prism at one side, the light bends, or refracts, through the angled surface. As it refracts, each color's wavelength bends at a slightly different angle. This is what separates the colors. A rainbow becomes visible!

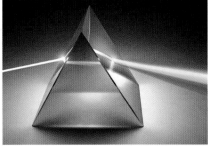

White light bending within a prism, separating the colors and projecting a rainbow

SIR ISAAC NEWTON

Sir Isaac Newton performing his experiment with sunbeams and prisms

Since ancient times, many scientists and philosophers had studied **prisms**. Many recognized that sunlight streaming through a **prism** created a rainbow. But British scientist Sir Isaac Newton made an amazing discovery in 1665. He set out to discover why these colors appeared, and always in the same order. Newton placed a prism on a table. Then he made a hole in his window shutter. This allowed only a small beam of sunlight to hit the prism. A rainbow appeared on the wall facing the window.

Newton did more experiments. He used another screen with a small hole to study each color in what he called the "**spectrum.**" Newton discovered each color was bent at a different angle. Others had believed that white light contained many colors. Newton's experiments proved it! He also proved that each color refracts at a different angle through a prism.

15

SEEING
COLOR

Your eyes are amazing organs. Working with your brain, they take in the world of colors around you.

There are many parts of the eye used to interpret color. First, light enters the eyeball through the **cornea**. Light passes through the cornea and enters the pupil. Then it makes its way to the retina at the back and sides

Rods see the shapes of the test tubes. Cones tell the brain the tubes hold orange liquid!

of the eye. Within the retina are **rods** and **cones**. Each eye has more than 100 million rods, which only detect gray. More than 5 million cones in each eye detect color. These cones are sensitive to bright light.

Photons in the light react with **pigments** inside the cones. Then the cones send a color-coded signal to the brain through the optic nerve. This is the eye's link to the brain. The brain then understands what colors you are seeing.

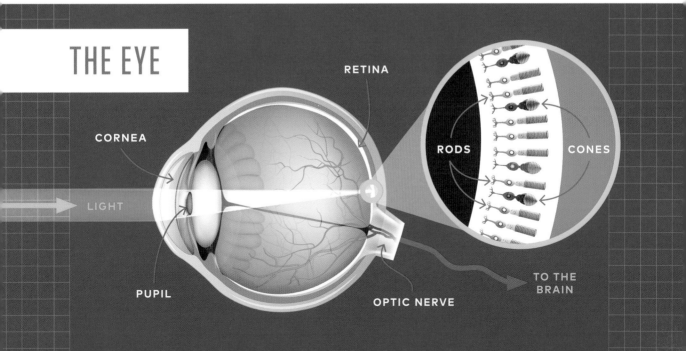

THE EYE

CORNEA

RETINA

RODS

CONES

LIGHT

PUPIL

OPTIC NERVE

TO THE BRAIN

WHAT'S ITS COLOR?

Seeing what color something is seems simple, right? But it's actually kind of tricky. Take an orange, for example. An orange isn't really orange. In fact, orange is the only color the fruit doesn't have!

We see objects in different colors. But those objects don't truly possess the colors we see. We have learned that objects reflect and absorb light. We do not see the colors that are absorbed. We see the color that is reflected.

Here's how it works. White light shines on an object. That object contains molecules of **pigments**. These molecules allow energy to transfer inside the object. The object absorbs some of the photons in the light. That means some of the light's colors are absorbed.

The colors that are not absorbed are reflected from the object. We see the object as having that reflected color. So when light hits an orange, all colors in the light are absorbed, except for the color orange. The orange light is reflected, and the color we see!

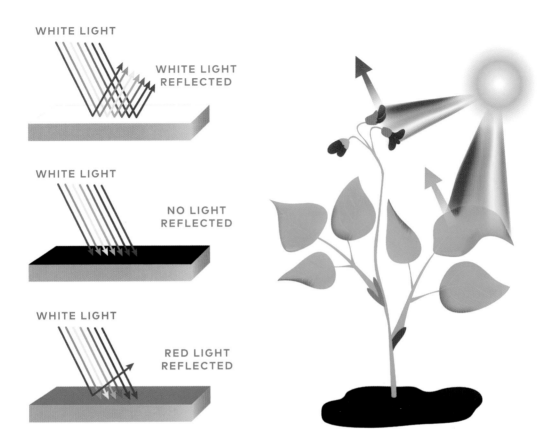

When all of visible light's colors are reflected, we see white.
We see black when all colors are absorbed. We see a surface or
object as a single color, such as red or green, when that color is
the only one reflected and not absorbed.

COLOR AND
HEAT

Reflection not only affects an object's color, but its temperature too. It's never a good idea to go barefoot on black asphalt in the summer. The hot asphalt can really hurt your feet. But do you know why the asphalt is hot? It is because of sunlight and color.

If the white paint used on its center lines were to cover this asphalt, its surface would absorb less heat.

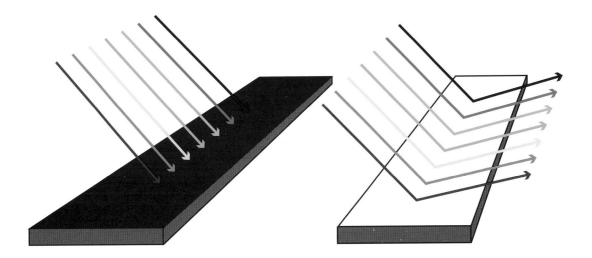

Along with color wavelengths, heat energy is either absorbed into or reflected off objects.

Remember, things that look black absorb all the colors of the **spectrum**. The colors they absorb are a form of energy. As light energy is absorbed, molecules inside the black object start moving more.

As they move, the molecules create heat. The light energy becomes heat energy. So, the more colors an object absorbs, the hotter it will get.

Since black absorbs all colors, black objects in the sunlight get really hot. Unlike black objects, white objects reflect all colors. Objects that look white stay much cooler in summer sunlight.

PIXELS AND PAINTS

The rainbow's colors mix to make white light. But what if you mixed seven colors of paint together? Would the paint turn white? Most likely it would be a **murky** brown-black color. So what's the difference?

Unlike light, paint contains **pigments**. Pigment colors are subtractive. This means that when colors are combined, the paint becomes darker. The primary colors for pigment are cyan blue, magenta red, and yellow. Mixed together, these colors produce black. Painters, poster designers, and illustrators use and mix pigment colors.

CHAPTER 6

Pigments mix, becoming darker

The additive color palette is called RGB, after its primary colors of red, green, and blue.

Colors of light react very differently than paint colors. Colors of light are additive. This means that when more than one is combined, brightness increases.

Red, green, and blue are the primary light colors used for mixing. Two of these colors added together are brighter than either one alone. When all three are mixed together, these colors are even brighter, producing white. Video artists, website designers, and theater lighting designers work with combinations of light color.

An example of mixing colors of light can be seen in television and computer screens. The screens start out black. When these machines are turned on, light is forced through their screens. The many-colored **pixels** form pictures.

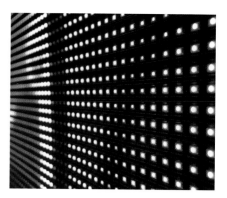

The black space between pixels, called "mesh," becomes invisible from far away.

Watch a music video on your computer. Or check out your favorite TV show. What do you see? Lots of different images you can easily recognize. But what if you looked really, really closely at the screen? You'd see millions of tiny pixels in combinations of just three different colors.

On screens, each pixel has a code. It gives a pixel a certain amount of red, blue, and green. The colors show through as light **illuminates** the screen. Up close, the pixels look like separate colored dots. From a distance though, the dots form a **complex** image.

RUSSELL KIRSCH

The world's first digital image, of Russell Kirsch's son, Walden.

In the 1950s, computers were very new. Only a select few had access to computers. Russell Kirsch was a scientist working for the US government at the time. He had access to the only programmable computer in the United States. Kirsch wondered how images could be shown on a computer screen. In 1957, he made the first digital image. It was a photo of his baby son. Kirsch used a device that turned the image into computer code. That code told the computer how to shade the **pixels** on the monitor. That first image was very fuzzy though. It only had 176 by 176 pixels. That is just a tiny fraction of the pixels we use today to create images on-screen.

NATURE'S
COLOR

The sky is something you see almost every day. But did you ever wonder why the sky is blue? Why isn't it yellow or green? It's because blue has a shorter **wavelength** than other colors in the **spectrum**. When sunlight hits Earth's atmosphere, it meets molecules. These molecules scatter light's waves. The shorter waves scatter more than longer waves. What we see is a beautiful blue sky.

Look around and you'll see many colors in nature. These colors are only possible because of light. A rainbow shows us all the colors contained within light. Objects show

26

What colors are absorbed in trees to make them appear green?

Visible light's variety of wavelengths create vibrant and colorful landscapes!

the colors they reflect from light. The human eye looks at an object. It perceives color to send color-coded messages to our brains. The many ways light travels, reflects, absorbs, and is perceived makes the world a very colorful place!

WATER RAINBOW

AN EXPERIMENT WITH LIGHT AND WATER

QUESTION

Can you create a rainbow by shining light on a mirror that is underwater?

RESEARCH

You've already learned rainbows are created when sunlight shines through a drop of water (see page 5). Can you create a **prism** using a larger amount of water? Here are some materials you will need to find out:

- shallow glass dish
- water
- white paper
- sunlight or flashlight
- small mirror

PREDICT

What will happen when the light shines through water? **Predict** what the light will do. Write it down.

TEST

1. Fill the dish halfway with water.

2. Set the mirror in the water. Lean it at an angle against the dish.

3. Let light shine on the part of the mirror that is underwater.

4. Hold the paper above the mirror. Move it at different angles until you see a rainbow appear on the paper.

ASSESS

Was your prediction correct? Why or why not? Why do you think you needed the mirror? What would happen if you used a different kind of liquid? Write down your thoughts. Then experiment again!

GLOSSARY

complex – having many parts, details, ideas, or functions.

cone – a cone-shaped receptor cell in the retina that allows the human eye to see color.

cornea – the transparent outer part of the human eye.

electromagnetic – relating to a magnetic field created by a current of electricity. Electromagnetic fields include radio waves and visible light.

electromagnetic radiation – a form of energy the human eye cannot see and which is released by certain electromagnetic processes.

emit – to give off or out.

illuminate – to light up or bring light to something.

murky – dark and cloudy.

nuclear fusion – the combining of two atomic nuclei to create a nucleus of greater mass.

pigment – a substance that gives color to something.

pixel – any of the small elements of brightness and color that create a picture when combined.

predict – to guess something ahead of time on the basis of observation, experience, or reasoning.

prism – a clear glass or plastic object with angles that separates the colors of the spectrum contained within light.

rod – a long, rod-shaped receptor cell in the retina that responds to dim light.

spectrum – the range of colors revealed in light through a rainbow or prism.

suncatcher – an ornament hung in a window and made of clear or colored glass.

transparent – clear or able to be seen through.

ultimately – finally, or at the end.

wavelength – the distance from one high point to the next high point in a wave of light or sound.

WEBSITES

To learn more about Science in Action, visit **booklinks.abdopublishing.com**. These links are routinely monitored and updated to provide the most current information available.

INDEX